Practical
Summer Food

p^3

This is a P³ Book
First published in 2003

P³
Queen Street House
4 Queen Street
Bath BA1 1HE, UK

ISBN: 1-40540-942-8

Printed in China

NOTE

Cup measurements in this book are for American cups.
This book also uses imperial and metric measurements. Follow the same units
of measurement throughout; do not mix imperial and metric.
All spoon measurements are level: teaspoons are assumed to be 5 ml, and
tablespoons are assumed to be 15 ml. Unless otherwise stated,
milk is assumed to be whole milk, eggs and individual vegetables such as potatoes
are medium, and pepper is freshly ground black pepper.

The nutritional information provided for each recipe is per serving or per person.
Optional ingredients, variations, or serving suggestions have not been
included in the calculations. The times given for each recipe are an approximate
guide only because the preparation times may differ according to the techniques used by
different people and the cooking times may vary as a result of the type of oven used.

Recipes using raw or very lightly cooked eggs should be
avoided by infants, the elderly, pregnant women, convalescents,
and anyone suffering from an illness.

Contents

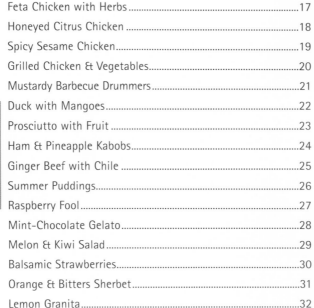

Introduction

Summertime is all about easy living, so when it comes to preparing meals, you want something light on effort yet lively on the taste buds. Fortunately, help and inspiration are at hand with this range of quick and easy, enticing recipes that will bring you the very best of the season. The key to successful summer cooking is to create dishes that capture the essence of the sun-ripened produce readily available in abundance and to let those full-blown flavors and aromas speak for themselves, from the fragrance of herbs, and the heady zest of citrus fruits, to the honeyed-wine scents and tastes of ripe summer berries.

Summer sizzling

Food grilled over hot coals in the balmy outdoors is the quintessential summer eating experience. A barbecue offers the perfect opportunity to relax and have fun with friends and family while enjoying the flavor of summer ingredients at their best, locked in by the heat and intensified by the smoke.

There are many different barbecue and outdoor grills to choose from in a variety of sizes, the smaller and lighter being portable or semiportable. Some have lids that completely cover the grill to create ovenlike conditions, with the temperature being controlled by vents. Gas and electric barbecue grills are becoming increasingly popular, since they heat up quickly, are easy to regulate, and the lava rock coals are self-cleaning.

Useful accessories

The following accessories will help make barbecuing trouble-free:

Long, insulated gloves or mitts These will protect your hands and forearms from the heat.

Long-handled tongs These are ideal for moving and spreading out briquettes or for positioning and turning foods on the rack. Choose a firm, sturdy pair.

Long-handled basting brush The length of the handle is the important factor here.

Hinged metal broiling racks These come in various shapes and sizes for holding different ingredients such as fish, meat, or vegetables, and allow the foods to be turned easily and without the risk of breaking up.

Skewers Metal skewers should be flat to prevent the food from slipping around when turning. Wooden skewers need to be soaked for at least 30 minutes before being used so that they do not catch fire.

Water spray gun Keep this handy at all times to douse any flareups if necessary, or for dampening down the coals if they are too hot. This is ideal for cleaning the surface of the grill rack between uses.

Tips for a successful barbecue

Choose a level, sheltered site for setting up the barbecue grill, well away from vegetation and buildings. If using a charcoal barbecue grill, always allow enough time for the outside of the coals to burn down to gray ash before cooking—at least 45 minutes, or half an hour for instant-lighting charcoal briquettes.

Brush the grill rack with vegetable oil, or use a vegetable oil spray, to prevent the foods from sticking to it and to aid cleaning. Position the rack about 2 inches/5 cm above the heat. To slow down the cooking, raise the height of the grill rack; if it is not adjustable, spread out the coals or move food to the edge where the heat will be less intense.

Use the outer portion of the grill for cooking thicker pieces of food.

When cooking kabobs, brush metal skewers with oil before using. Choose a combination of ingredients that will cook at the same rate and in the same time and leave a small, even amount of space in between; do not pack them tightly or they may not cook through properly.

Vegetables and other foods can be wrapped in foil with seasonings and a little bouillon or wine and cooked on the grill rack to enclose all their juices and leave them tender. Be sure to use heavy-duty aluminum foil for this purpose.

Choose only good-quality, lean cuts of meat for grilling to ensure tenderness. Trim most of the fat from around steaks or chops to prevent flareups but leave a little to lubricate the meat.

Hardwood chips, such as hickory, or fruitwood chips, such as apple or cherry, contribute an extra smoky quality to grilled foods. Soak the chips for about an hour (longer if using chunks) before sprinkling over the hot coals, to prevent them from burning.

Al fresco food

Picnics are another marvelous way of enjoying summer food in whatever environment takes your fancy, from the beach or woods to your own backyard.

To keep foods cool in high temperatures, always transport them in a cooler. A full cooler will keep foods colder than one that it is partially filled, but the latter can be topped up with extra ice packs or large chunks of ice—these stay frozen longer than smaller ice cubes. Position the cooler in the shade. Keep chilled soups, or fruit salads, ice-cold by storing them in wide-necked vacuum flasks.

To serve foods warm, put them into airtight containers, wrap tightly in heavy-duty aluminum foil, then wrap again in several sheets of newspaper.

To keep salads crisp, do not add the dressing until you are ready to serve. Transport the dressing in a screw-top jar and simply shake before pouring over the salad.

Make desserts in individual servings, rather than as one dish, which are less space-consuming and much easier to serve at the picnic site.

Summer celebrations

There is no need to labor over preparing and cooking elaborate dishes for a celebratory meal. With a few stylish presentation ideas, you can elevate simple summer classics into studies in elegant sophistication.

Herb leaves and flowers and other edible summer flowers, such as mint leaves, chive flowers, rose petals or buds, jasmine flowers, pansies, and nasturtiums, can be used decoratively and for an additional touch of fragrant flavor. Wash thoroughly and scatter over salads or use to decorate fruit salads and other desserts. Herbs such as

parsley and tarragon can be finely chopped and beaten into softened butter, then rolled out and shapes stamped out with fancy cutters, to garnish meat and fish dishes. Pretty blue borage flowers, which have a distinctive cucumberlike flavor, or other herb flowers and leaves, can be added to half-filled ice-cube trays, topped up with water, and then frozen, to add to punches and coolers. Or why not make a whole ice bowl by adding herb flowers to the gap between a small and medium-size freezerproof glass bowl placed one inside the other and taped into position, filled up with water, and then frozen? This is ideal for presenting sherbets and ice creams or fruit salads.

Rice salads, or a rice accompaniment, can also be imaginatively presented, pressed into individual fluted molds or one large ring mold, and upturned onto individual plates or a serving platter to make an attractive centerpiece.

KEY	
	Simplicity level 1–3 (1 easiest, 3 slightly harder)
	Preparation time
	Cooking time

Garlic & Almond Soup

This pretty, pale, chilled soup looks beautiful with its unusual garnish of sliced white grapes and a swirl of olive oil.

NUTRITIONAL INFORMATION

Calories 513	Sugars 3g
Protein 15g	Fat 34g
Carbohydrate . . .40g	Saturates 4g

30 mins, plus chilling   0 mins

SERVES 4–6

I N G R E D I E N T S

14 oz/400 g day-old French bread, sliced

4 large garlic cloves

4 cups water, chilled

3–4 tbsp sherry vinegar

6 tbsp extra-virgin olive oil

2 cups ground almonds

sea salt and pepper

T O   G A R N I S H

seedless white grapes, chilled and sliced

pepper

extra-virgin olive oil

1   Tear the bread into small pieces and put in a bowl. Pour over enough cold water to cover and soak for 10–15 minutes. Using your hands, squeeze the bread dry. Transfer the moist bread to a food processor.

COOK'S TIP

Instead of grapes, serve with Garlic Croûtons and diced vegetables (see the Gazpacho recipe opposite). Alternatively, sprinkle with a dusting of paprika or very finely chopped fresh parsley just before serving.

2   Cut the garlic cloves in half lengthwise and use the tip of the knife to remove the pale green or white cores. Add to the food processor with 3 tablespoons of the sherry vinegar and 1 cup of the water, and process until blended. Add the oil and ground almonds and blend.

3   With the motor running, slowly pour in the remaining water, until a smooth soup forms. Add extra sherry vinegar to taste, and season with salt and pepper. Transfer the soup to a bowl, cover, and chill in the refrigerator for at least 4 hours.

4   To serve, adjust the seasoning. Ladle into bowls and float grapes on top. Garnish each with a sprinkling of pepper and a swirl of olive oil. Serve while still very cold.

Iced Gazpacho

This delicious soup, with its brightly colored garnish of bell peppers, cucumber, and scallions, is perfect to serve at a summer lunch party.

NUTRITIONAL INFORMATION

Calories 164	Sugars 7g
Protein 3g	Fat 12g
Carbohydrate ...13g	Saturates 3g

20 mins, plus chilling   5 mins

SERVES 4–6

INGREDIENTS

2 ripe red bell peppers

1 cucumber

1 lb/450 g large, juicy tomatoes, skinned, seeded, and coarsely chopped

4 tbsp olive oil

2 tbsp sherry vinegar

salt and pepper

GARLIC CROUTONS

2 tbsp olive oil

1 garlic clove, halved

2 slices bread, crusts removed, cut into ¼-inch/5-mm cubes

sea salt

TO GARNISH

green bell pepper, diced

red bell pepper, diced

cucumber, seeded and finely diced

scallions, chopped

ice cubes

sprigs of fresh parsley, or other herbs

1 Cut the bell peppers in half and remove the cores and seeds, then chop coarsely. Peel the cucumber, cut it in half lengthwise, then cut into fourths. Remove the seeds with a teaspoon, then chop the flesh coarsely.

2 Put the chopped red bell peppers, cucumber, and tomatoes with the olive oil and sherry vinegar in a food processor and process until smooth. Season the soup with salt and pepper to taste. Transfer to a bowl, cover, and chill for at least 4 hours.

3 Meanwhile, make the garlic croûtons. Heat the oil in a skillet over medium-high heat. Add the garlic and sauté, stirring, for 2 minutes to flavor the oil.

4 Lift out and discard the garlic. Add the diced bread and cook until golden on all sides. Drain well on crumpled paper towels and sprinkle with sea salt. Store in an airtight container if not using at once.

5 To serve, place each of the vegetable garnishes in bowls for guests to add to their soup. Taste the soup and adjust the seasoning if necessary. Put ice cubes into soup bowls then ladle over the soup. Top with sprigs of parsley and serve at once.

Pan Bagna

A cornucopia of the best flavors of the Mediterranean, this French sandwich never follows a set recipe. Treat this version as a suggestion.

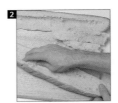
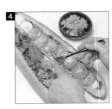
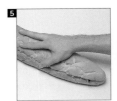

NUTRITIONAL INFORMATION

Calories	422	Sugars	4g
Protein	27g	Fat	16g
Carbohydrate	44g	Saturates	3g

15 mins, plus 3 hrs chilling   0 mins

SERVES 4

INGREDIENTS

16-inch/40-cm long loaf of country bread, thicker than a French baguette

about 2 tbsp fruity extra-virgin olive oil

black or green olive tapenade, for spreading (optional)

FILLING

2 eggs, hard-cooked and shelled

1¾ oz/50 g anchovy fillets in oil

about ⅔ cup flavored olives of your choice

lettuce or arugula leaves, rinsed and patted dry

about 4 plum tomatoes, sliced

7 oz/200 g canned tuna in brine, well drained and flaked

1 Slice the eggs. Drain the anchovy fillets, then cut them in half lengthwise. Pit the olives and slice in half.

2 Slice the loaf in half lengthwise. Pull out about ½ inch/1 cm of the crumb from the centers, leaving a border all around both halves.

3 Generously brush both halves with olive oil. Spread with tapenade, if you like a strong flavor. Arrange lettuce or arugula leaves on the bottom half.

4 Add layers of hard-cooked egg slices, tomato slices, olives, anchovies, and tuna, sprinkling with olive oil and adding lettuce or arugula leaves between the layers. Make the filling as thick as you like.

5 Place the other bread half on top and press down firmly. Wrap tightly in plastic wrap and place on a board or plate that will fit in your refrigerator. Weigh it down and chill for several hours. To serve, slice into 4 equal portions, tying with string to secure in place, if desired.

VARIATION

Other typical Mediterranean fillings for a Pan Bagna include crushed garlic, red or green bell peppers, young fava beans, gherkins, artichoke hearts, Spanish onions, fresh herbs, and pitted olives.

Plain Strained Yogurt

Smooth and creamy, this yogurt makes a refreshing start to hot days, spread on pitas for breakfast, or as a dip for an afternoon snack.

NUTRITIONAL INFORMATION

Calories 32	Sugars 3g
Protein 2g	Fat 1g
Carbohydrate 3g	Saturates 1g

 36½ hrs   0 mins

MAKES ABOUT 2¼ CUPS

I N G R E D I E N T S

4 cups plain yogurt

½ tsp salt

O P T I O N A L   T O P P I N G S

fruity extra-virgin olive oil

orange blossom honey or lavender honey

coriander seeds, crushed

paprika

very finely chopped fresh mint or cilantro

finely grated lemon rind

1 Place a 50 x 30-inch/125 x 75-cm piece of cheesecloth in a pan, cover with water, and bring to a boil. Remove the pan from the heat and, using a wooden spoon, lift out the cheesecloth. Wearing rubber gloves to protect your hands, wring the cheesecloth dry.

2 Fold the cheesecloth into a double layer and use it to line a colander or strainer set over a large bowl. Put the yogurt in a bowl and stir in the salt, then spoon into the center of the cheesecloth.

3 Tie the cheesecloth so it is suspended above the bowl. If your sink is deep enough, gather up the corners of the cheesecloth and tie it to the faucet. If not, lay a broom handle across 2 chairs and put the bowl between the chairs. Tie the cheesecloth to the broom handle. Remove the colander or strainer and let the yogurt drain into the bowl for at least 12 hours.

4 Transfer the yogurt to a nylon strainer placed in a bowl. Cover lightly with plastic wrap and refrigerate for 24 hours, until soft and creamy. The yogurt will keep in the refrigerator for up to 5 days.

5 To serve, taste and add extra salt if needed. Spoon the yogurt into a bowl and sprinkle with the topping of your choice or a combination of toppings.

Caesar Salad

This salad was the invention of a chef at Caesar's, a restaurant in Tijuana, Mexico. It has rightly earned an international reputation.

NUTRITIONAL INFORMATION

Calories	589	Sugars	.........3g
Protein	........11g	Fat	..........50g
Carbohydrate	...24g	Saturates	.......9g

🍴 🍴

🥗 25 mins   🕐 15–20 mins

SERVES 4

INGREDIENTS

1 large romaine lettuce, or 2 Boston or Bibb lettuces

4 canned anchovies in oil, drained and halved lengthwise

Parmesan shavings, to garnish

DRESSING

2 garlic cloves, crushed

1½ tsp Dijon mustard

1 tsp Worcestershire sauce

4 canned anchovies in olive oil, drained and chopped

1 egg yolk

1 tbsp lemon juice

⅔ cup olive oil

4 tbsp freshly grated Parmesan cheese

salt and pepper

CROUTONS

4 thick slices day-old bread

2 tbsp olive oil

1 garlic clove, crushed

1 First, make the dressing. Put the garlic, mustard, Worcestershire sauce, anchovies, egg yolk, lemon juice, and seasoning into a food processor or blender and process for 30 seconds, until foaming. Add the olive oil, drop by drop, until the mixture begins to thicken, then in a steady stream so that all the oil is incorporated. Scrape out of the food processor or blender. Add a little hot water if the dressing is too thick. Stir in the grated Parmesan cheese. Taste for seasoning and set aside in the refrigerator until required.

2 For the croûtons, cut the bread into ½-inch/1-cm cubes. Toss with the olive oil and garlic in a bowl. Spread out on a cookie sheet in a single layer. Bake in a preheated oven, 350°F/180°C, for 15–20 minutes, stirring occasionally, until the croûtons are browned and crisp. Remove from the oven and set aside to cool.

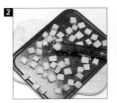

3 Separate the lettuce into individual leaves and wash and spin dry in a salad spinner or pat dry on paper towels (excess moisture will dilute the dressing.) Transfer to a plastic bag and place in the refrigerator until needed.

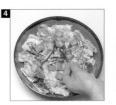

4 To assemble the salad, tear the lettuce into pieces and place a large serving bowl. Add the dressing and toss well. Top with the halved anchovies, croûtons, and Parmesan shavings. Serve immediately.

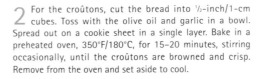

Tuna Niçoise Salad

This is a classic version of the French salade niçoise. It is a substantial salad, suitable for a lunch or light summer supper.

NUTRITIONAL INFORMATION

Calories	109	Sugars	.......1.1g
Protein	........7.2g	Fat	.........7.0g
Carbohydrate	...4.8g	Saturates	.....1.2g

10 mins   20 mins

SERVES 4

INGREDIENTS

4 eggs

1 lb/450 g new potatoes

4 oz/115 g small green beans, trimmed
and halved

2 tuna steaks, about 6 oz/175 g each

6 tbsp olive oil, plus extra for brushing

1 garlic clove, crushed

1½ tsp Dijon mustard

2 tsp lemon juice

2 tbsp chopped fresh basil

2 Boston or Bibb lettuces

7 oz/200 g cherry tomatoes, halved

6 oz/175 g cucumber, peeled, cut in half,
and sliced

2 oz/55 g pitted black olives

2 oz/55 g canned anchovies in olive
oil, drained

salt and pepper

2 Cook the potatoes in lightly salted boiling water for 10–12 minutes, until tender. Add the beans 3 minutes before the end of the cooking time. Drain both vegetables well and refresh under cold water. Drain well again.

3 Wash and dry the tuna steaks. Brush with a little olive oil and season to taste. Cook on a preheated ridged griddle for 2–3 minutes each side, until just tender but still slightly pink in the center. Set aside to rest.

4 Whisk together the garlic, mustard, lemon juice, basil, and seasoning. Whisk in the remaining olive oil.

5 To assemble the salad, break apart the lettuces and tear into large pieces. Divide among individual serving plates. Next, add the potatoes and beans, tomatoes, cucumber, and olives. Toss lightly together. Shell the eggs and cut into fourths lengthwise. Arrange these on top of the salad. Scatter the anchovies over the top.

6 Flake the tuna steaks and arrange on the salad. Pour over the dressing and serve.

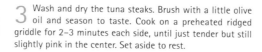

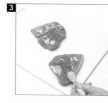

1 Bring a small pan of water to a boil. Add the eggs and then cook for 7–9 minutes from when the water returns to a boil—7 minutes for a slightly soft center or 9 minutes for a firm center. Drain and refresh under cold running water. Set aside.

Orange & Fennel Salad

Fresh, juicy oranges and the sharp anise flavor of fennel combine to make this refreshing Spanish salad.

NUTRITIONAL INFORMATION

Calories	136	Sugars	........19g
Protein	.........3g	Fat	..........6g
Carbohydrate	...19g	Saturates	.......1g

 30 mins   0 mins

SERVES 4

INGREDIENTS

4 large oranges

1 large bulb fennel

2 tsp fennel seeds

2 tbsp extra-virgin olive oil

freshly squeezed orange juice, to taste

fresh parsley, finely chopped, to garnish

1 Using a small serrated knife, remove the rind and pith from 1 orange, cutting carefully from the top to the bottom of the orange so it retains its shape. Work over a small bowl to catch the juices.

2 Peel the remaining oranges the same way, reserving all the juices. Cut the oranges horizontally into ¼-inch/5-mm slices and arrange in an attractive serving bowl; reserve the juices.

VARIATION

Replace the fennel with a finely sliced onion or a large bunch of scallions, finely chopped. This version is from Spain, where orange-colored oranges would be used, but in Sicily the dish is made with blood-red oranges.

3 Cut the fronds from the fennel bulb, cut the bulb in half lengthwise, and then into fourths. Cut crosswise into very thin slices. Immediately place in the bowl of oranges and toss with a little of the reserved juice to prevent discoloration.

4 Sprinkle the fennel seeds over the oranges and sliced fennel.

5 Whisk the olive oil with the remaining reserved orange juice, plus extra fresh orange juice to taste. Pour over the oranges and fennel and toss gently. Cover with plastic wrap and chill, until ready to serve.

6 Just before serving, remove from the refrigerator and sprinkle with parsley. Serve chilled.

Bean Curd Skewers

Although bean curd is rather bland on its own, it develops
a fabulous flavor when it is marinated in garlic and herbs.

NUTRITIONAL INFORMATION		
Calories 149	Sugars 5g	
Protein 13g	Fat 9g	
Carbohydrate 5g	Saturates 1g	

🥄 🥄 🥄

🍋 40 mins   🕐 15 mins

SERVES 4

I N G R E D I E N T S

12 oz/350 g bean curd

1 red bell pepper

1 yellow bell pepper

2 zucchini

8 white mushrooms

lemon slices, to garnish

M A R I N A D E

grated rind and juice of ½ lemon

1 garlic clove, crushed

½ tsp chopped fresh rosemary

½ tsp chopped fresh thyme

1 tbsp walnut oil

1 To make the marinade, combine the
lemon rind and juice, garlic, rosemary,
thyme, and oil in a shallow dish.

2 Drain the bean curd, pat it dry on
paper towels, and cut it into squares
with a sharp knife. Add to the marinade
and toss to coat. Cover and set aside to
marinate for 20–30 minutes.

3 Meanwhile, seed and cut the bell
peppers into 1-inch/2.5-cm pieces.
Blanch in boiling water for 4 minutes,
refresh in cold water, and drain.

4 Using a canelle knife or potato peeler,
remove strips of peel from the
zucchini. Cut the zucchini into 1-inch/
2.5-cm chunks.

5 Remove the bean curd from the
marinade, reserving the liquid. Thread
it onto 8 skewers, alternating with the bell
peppers, zucchini, and mushrooms.

6 Grill the skewers over medium hot
coals for about 6 minutes, turning
and basting with the reserved marinade.
Alternatively, cook under a preheated
broiler. Transfer the skewers to warmed
individual serving plates, garnish with
slices of lemon, and serve.

Poached Rainbow Trout

This colorful, flavorsome dish can be served cold and therefore makes a lovely summer lunch or *al fresco* supper dish.

NUTRITIONAL INFORMATION

Calories	99	Sugars	.......1.1g
Protein	........5.7g	Fat	..........6.3g
Carbohydrate	...3.7g	Saturates	.......1g

🗪 🗪 🗪

🍲 25 mins   🕐 1 hr

SERVES 4

I N G R E D I E N T S

3 lb/1.3 kg rainbow trout fillets

1 lb 9 oz/700 g new potatoes

3 scallions, finely chopped

1 egg, hard-cooked and chopped

C O U R T - B O U I L L O N

3½ cups cold water

3½ cups dry white wine

3 tbsp white wine vinegar

2 large carrots, coarsely chopped

1 onion, coarsely chopped

2 celery stalks, coarsely chopped

2 leeks, coarsely chopped

2 garlic cloves, coarsely chopped

2 fresh bay leaves

4 sprigs of fresh parsley

4 sprigs of fresh thyme

6 black peppercorns

1 tsp salt

M A Y O N N A I S E

1 egg yolk

1 tsp Dijon mustard

1 tsp white wine vinegar

2 oz/55 g watercress or baby spinach leaves, chopped

1 cup light olive oil

salt and pepper

1 First make the court-bouillon. Place all the ingredients in a large pan and bring to a boil over low heat. Cover and simmer for about 30 minutes. Strain the liquid through a fine strainer into a clean pan. Bring to a boil again and then simmer rapidly, uncovered, for 15–20 minutes, until the court-bouillon is reduced to about 2½ cups.

2 Place the trout in a large skillet. Add the court-bouillon and bring to a boil over low heat. Remove from the heat and set the fish aside in the liquid to cool.

3 Meanwhile, make the mayonnaise. Put the egg yolk, Dijon mustard, white wine vinegar, watercress or spinach, and salt and pepper to taste into a food processor or blender and process for 30 seconds, until foaming. Begin adding the olive oil, drop by drop, until the mixture begins to thicken. Continue adding the oil in a slow, steady stream, until it is all incorporated. Add a little hot water if the mixture seems too thick. Season to taste and set aside.

4 Cook the potatoes in plenty of lightly salted boiling water for about 12–15 minutes, until soft and tender. Drain well and refresh them under cold running water. Set the potatoes aside until cold.

5 When the potatoes are cold, cut them in half, if they are very large, and toss thoroughly with the mayonnaise, finely chopped scallions, and hard-cooked egg.

6 Carefully lift the fish from the poaching liquid and drain on paper towels. Carefully pull the skin away from each of the trout fillets. Serve immediately with the potato salad, or let cool and serve chilled.

Red Snapper & Coconut Loaf

This fish and coconut loaf is ideal to take along on picnics, because it can be served cold as well as hot.

NUTRITIONAL INFORMATION

Calories 138	Sugars 12g	
Protein 11g	Fat 1g	
Carbohydrate ...23g	Saturates 0g	

15 mins   1¼ hrs

SERVES 4–6

INGREDIENTS

8 oz/225 g red snapper fillets, skinned

2 tomatoes, seeded and finely chopped

2 green bell peppers, finely chopped

1 onion, finely chopped

1 fresh red chile, finely chopped

2¾ cups bread crumbs

2½ cups coconut liquid (see step 2, below)

salt and pepper

HOT PEPPER SAUCE

½ cup tomato catsup

1 tsp West Indian hot pepper sauce

¼ tsp hot mustard

TO GARNISH

twists of fresh lemon

sprigs of fresh chervil

 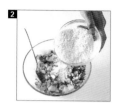 

1 Finely chop the fish and mix with the tomatoes, bell peppers, onion, and fresh chile.

2 Stir in the bread crumbs, coconut liquid, and seasoning. If using fresh coconut, use a hammer and the tip of a sturdy knife to poke out the "eyes" in the top and pour out the liquid.

3 Grease a 1 lb 2-oz/500-g loaf pan and line the bottom. Add the fish mixture.

4 Bake in a preheated oven, 400°F/200°C, for 1–1¼ hours, until set.

5 To make the hot pepper sauce, combine the tomato catsup, West Indian hot pepper sauce, and mustard, until smooth and creamy.

6 To serve, cut the loaf into slices, arrange on a serving platter, garnish with lemon twists and chervil, and serve hot or cold with the sauce.

COOK'S TIP

Be careful when preparing chiles because the juices can irritate the skin, especially the face. Wash your hands after handling them or wear clean rubber gloves to prepare them if preferred.

Grilled Monkfish

Monkfish cooks very well on a barbecue because it is a firm-fleshed fish. Make sure that you remove the membrane before cooking.

NUTRITIONAL INFORMATION	
Calories 219	Sugars 0g
Protein 28g	Fat 12g
Carbohydrate 1g	Saturates 2g

2¼ hrs   5–6 mins

SERVES 4

INGREDIENTS

4 tbsp olive oil

grated rind of 1 lime

2 tsp Thai fish sauce

2 garlic cloves, crushed

1 tsp grated fresh gingerroot

2 tbsp chopped fresh basil

1 lb 9 oz/700 g monkfish fillet, cut into chunks

2 limes, each cut into 6 wedges

salt and pepper

1 Combine the olive oil, lime rind, fish sauce, garlic, grated ginger, and basil in a nonmetallic bowl. Season to taste with salt and pepper and set aside.

2 Wash the fish chunks and pat dry with paper towels. Add them to the marinade and mix well to coat. Cover and set aside in the refrigerator to marinate for 2 hours, stirring occasionally.

3 If you are using bamboo skewers, soak them in cold water for 30 minutes to prevent them from charring.

4 Lift the monkfish pieces from the marinade with a slotted spoon and thread them onto the skewers, alternating with the lime wedges.

5 Transfer the skewers, either to a hot barbecue or to a preheated ridged griddle pan. Cook for 5–6 minutes, turning regularly, until the fish is tender. Serve the skewers immediately.

VARIATION

You could use any type of white fleshed fish for this recipe but sprinkle the pieces with salt and leave for 2 hours to firm the flesh, before rinsing, drying, and then adding to the marinade.

Feta Chicken with Herbs

Chicken goes well with most savory herbs, especially during the summer, when fresh herbs are at their best.

NUTRITIONAL INFORMATION

Calories 283   Sugars 5g
Protein . . . . .25g   Fat 15g
Carbohydrate . . .14g   Saturates 2g

15–20 mins   25–30 mins

SERVES 4

INGREDIENTS

8 skinless, boneless chicken thighs

2 tbsp each chopped fresh thyme, rosemary, and oregano

4½ oz/125 g feta cheese

1 tbsp milk

2 tbsp all-purpose flour

salt and pepper

thyme, rosemary, and oregano, to garnish

TOMATO SAUCE

1 medium onion, coarsely chopped

1 garlic clove, crushed

1 tbsp olive oil

4 medium plum tomatoes, cut into fourths

sprig each of thyme, rosemary, and oregano

1 Spread out the chicken thighs, smooth side downward.

2 Divide the herbs among the chicken thighs, then cut the cheese into eight sticks. Place one stick of cheese in the center of each chicken thigh. Season well, then roll up the thighs to enclose the cheese.

3 Place the chicken thighs in an ovenproof pan, brush them with milk, and dust with flour to coat.

4 Bake in a preheated oven, 375°F/190°C, for 25–30 minutes, or until golden brown. The juices should run clear and not pink when the chicken is pierced with a skewer in the thickest part.

5 Meanwhile, to make the sauce, cook the onion and garlic in the oil, stirring, until softened and starting to brown.

6 Add the tomatoes, lower the heat, cover, and simmer for 15–20 minutes, or until soft.

7 Add the herbs, then transfer to a food processor and blend to a paste. Press through a strainer to make a smooth, rich sauce. Season and serve the sauce with the chicken, garnished with herbs.

Honeyed Citrus Chicken

This lowfat recipe is great for summer entertaining. If you cut the chicken in half and press it flat you can roast it in under an hour.

NUTRITIONAL INFORMATION

Calories ....288 Sugars 32g
Protein ....30g Fat 6g
Carbohydrate ...32g Saturates 1g

15–20 mins   45–50 mins

SERVES 4

INGREDIENTS

4 lb 8 oz/2 kg chicken

2 oranges, cut into wedges

salt and pepper

sprigs of fresh tarragon, to garnish

MARINADE

1¼ cups orange juice

3 tbsp cider vinegar

3 tbsp honey

2 tbsp chopped fresh tarragon

SAUCE

handful of tarragon sprigs, chopped

1 cup fat-free fromage frais

2 tbsp orange juice

1 tsp honey

2¼ oz/60 g stuffed olives, chopped

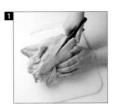

1 Put the chicken on a cutting board with the breast downward. Cut through the bottom part of the carcass using poultry shears or heavy kitchen scissors, making sure not to cut right through to the breast bone below.

2 Rinse the chicken with cold water, drain, and place on a board with the skin side uppermost. Press the chicken flat, then cut off the leg ends.

3 Thread two long wooden skewers through the bird to keep it flat. Season the skin.

4 Mix all the marinade ingredients in a shallow, nonmetallic dish. Add the chicken. Cover and chill for 4 hours, turning the chicken several times.

5 To make the sauce, mix all the ingredients and season. Spoon into a serving dish, cover, and chill.

6 Transfer the chicken and marinade to a roasting pan, open out the chicken, and place skin-side downward. Tuck the orange wedges around the chicken and roast in a preheated oven, 400°F/200°C, for 25 minutes. Turn the chicken over and roast for another 20–30 minutes. Baste until the chicken is browned and the juices run clear when pierced with a skewer. Garnish with tarragon and serve with the sauce.

Spicy Sesame Chicken

This is a quick and easy recipe for the broiler or barbecue grill, perfect for lunch or to eat outdoors on a picnic.

NUTRITIONAL INFORMATION

Calories 110   Sugars 3g
Protein . . . . .15g   Fat 4g
Carbohydrate . . . .3g   Saturates 1g

 5 mins   15 mins

SERVES 4

INGREDIENTS

4 chicken quarters

⅔ cup lowfat plain yogurt

finely grated rind and juice of 1 small lemon

2 tsp medium-hot curry paste

1 tbsp sesame seeds

TO SERVE

fresh salad

nan bread

wedges of fresh lemon

1 Remove the skin from the chicken and slash the flesh at intervals with a sharp knife.

2 Combine the yogurt, lemon rind and lemon juice, and curry paste.

3 Spread the mixture over the chicken and arrange on a foil-lined broiler pan or cookie sheet.

4 Place on a barbecue grill or under a preheated broiler and cook, turning once, for 12–15 minutes, until golden and cooked. Test by piercing the thickest part with a skewer; the juices should run clear. Just before the end of the cooking time, sprinkle with the sesame seeds.

5 Serve with a fresh salad, nan bread, and lemon wedges.

VARIATION

Poppy seeds, fennel seeds, or cumin seeds, or a mixture of all three, can also be used to sprinkle over the chicken.

Grilled Chicken & Vegetables

Grilling is a quick, healthy cooking method, ideal for sealing in the juices of chicken breasts, and a marvelous way to cook summer vegetables.

NUTRITIONAL INFORMATION	
Calories 611	Sugars 11g
Protein 43g	Fat 21g
Carbohydrate . . .66g	Saturates 3g

15 mins, plus 1 hr draining/marinating — 25 mins

SERVES 4

I N G R E D I E N T S

1 small eggplant, sliced

2 garlic cloves, crushed

finely grated zest of ½ lemon

1 tbsp chopped fresh mint

6 tbsp olive oil, plus extra for brushing/drizzling

4 boneless chicken breasts

2 medium zucchini, sliced

1 medium red bell pepper, cut into fourths

1 small bulb of fennel, thickly sliced

1 large red onion, thickly sliced

1 small ciabatta loaf or 1 French baguette, sliced

salt and pepper

1 Place the eggplant slices in a colander and sprinkle with salt. Stand over a bowl to drain for 30 minutes, then rinse and dry. This will draw out all of the bitter juices.

2 Mix together the garlic, lemon zest, mint, and olive oil, and season.

3 Slash the chicken breasts at intervals with a sharp knife. Spoon over about half of the oil mixture and stir to combine.

4 Combine the eggplant slices and the remaining vegetables, then toss them in the remaining oil mixture. Let the chicken and vegetables marinate for about 30 minutes.

5 Cook the chicken and vegetables under a preheated hot broiler or on a barbecue grill for about 20 minutes, turning them occasionally to prevent them from burning and sticking, until they are golden brown and tender. Alternatively, cook them in a ridged grill pan on the stove.

6 Brush the bread slices with olive oil and broil or grill, until golden.

7 Drizzle a little olive oil over the chicken and vegetables and serve hot or cold with the toasted bread.

Mustardy Barbecue Drummers

Great for grills, or for simple summer lunches and picnics, this is an easy and tasty recipe for chicken drumsticks.

NUTRITIONAL INFORMATION

Calories 394	Sugars 5g	
Protein 40g	Fat 27g	
Carbohydrate 3g	Saturates 8g	

10–15 mins   25 mins

SERVES 4

I N G R E D I E N T S

10 slices smoked streaky bacon

1 garlic clove, peeled and finely chopped

3 tbsp whole-grain mustard

4 tbsp fresh brown bread crumbs

8 chicken drumsticks

1 tbsp sunflower oil

sprigs of fresh parsley, to garnish

1 Chop two of the bacon slices into small pieces and dry cook in a pan for 3–4 minutes, stirring so that the bacon does not stick to the bottom. Remove from the heat and stir in the garlic, 2 tablespoons of the wholegrain mustard, and the bread crumbs.

2 Using your fingers, carefully loosen the skin from each drumstick, being careful not to tear the skin. Spoon a little of the mustard stuffing under each flap of skin, smoothing the skins over firmly after you have inserted the stuffing.

3 Wrap a bacon slice around each drumstick, and secure with toothpicks.

4 Mix together the remaining mustard and the oil, brush over the chicken drumsticks, and cook on a preheated moderately hot barbecue or under a broiler for about 25 minutes, until there is no trace of pink in the juices when the thickest part of the chicken is pierced with a skewer.

5 Garnish with sprigs of fresh parsley and serve hot or cold.

COOK'S TIP

Do not cook the chicken over the hottest part of the barbecue or the outside may be charred before the center is cooked.

Duck with Mangoes

Use fresh mangoes in this recipe for a terrific flavor and color. If they are unavailable, use canned mangoes and rinse them before using.

NUTRITIONAL INFORMATION

Calories 235	Sugars 6g	
Protein 23g	Fat 14g	
Carbohydrate 6g	Saturates 2g	

🕙 5 mins   🕙 35 mins

SERVES 4

I N G R E D I E N T S

2 ripe mangoes

1¼ cups chicken bouillon

2 garlic cloves, crushed

1 tsp grated fresh gingerroot

2 large, skinless duck breasts, about 8 oz/225 g each

3 tbsp vegetable oil

1 tsp wine vinegar

1 tsp light soy sauce

1 leek, sliced

chopped fresh parsley, to garnish

1 Peel the mangoes and cut the flesh from each side of the pits. Cut the flesh into strips.

2 Put half of the mango pieces and the chicken bouillon in a food processor and process until smooth. Alternatively, press half of the mangoes through a fine strainer and mix with the bouillon.

3 Rub the garlic and ginger over the duck breasts. Heat the oil in a preheated wok and cook the duck breasts, turning frequently, until sealed. Reserve the oil in the wok and remove the duck.

4 Place the duck breasts on a rack set over a roasting pan and cook in a preheated oven, 425°F/220°C, for about 20 minutes, until the duck is cooked through and tender.

5 Meanwhile, place the mango and bouillon mixture in a pan and add the wine vinegar and light soy sauce.

6 Bring the mixture to a boil and cook over high heat, stirring constantly, until reduced by half.

7 Heat the oil reserved in the wok and stir-fry the sliced leek and remaining mango for 1 minute. Remove from the wok, transfer to a serving dish, and keep warm until required.

8 Slice the cooked duck breasts and arrange the slices on top of the leek and mango mixture. Pour the sauce over the duck slices, garnish with chopped parsley, and serve immediately.

Prosciutto with Fruit

In this classic Italian dish, the slightly salty flavor of air-cured prosciutto provides a marvelous contrast to the sweet fresh fruit.

NUTRITIONAL INFORMATION

Calories .... 198 Sugars 13g
Protein .... 16g Fat 10g
Carbohydrate ... 13g Saturates 3g

10 mins 10 mins

SERVES 4

INGREDIENTS

1 cantaloupe or charentais melon

4 ripe, fresh figs (optional)

12 wafer-thin slices prosciutto

about 4 tsp olive oil, for drizzling

pepper

sprigs of fresh parsley, to garnish

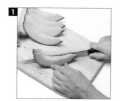

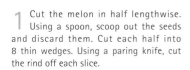

1 Cut the melon in half lengthwise. Using a spoon, scoop out the seeds and discard them. Cut each half into 8 thin wedges. Using a paring knife, cut the rind off each slice.

2 Cut the stems off the figs, if using, but do not peel them. Stand the figs upright with the pointed end upward. Cut each into fourths without cutting all the way through, so you can open them out into attractive "flowers."

3 Arrange 3–4 slices of prosciutto on individual serving plates and top with the melon slices and fig "flowers," if using. Alternatively, arrange the melon slices on the plates and completely cover with the prosciutto; add the figs, if using.

4 Drizzle with olive oil, then grind a little pepper over the top. Garnish with parsley and serve at once.

COOK'S TIP

For an attractive presentation, you can also prepare all the ingredients on one large serving platter and let guests help themselves.

Ham & Pineapple Kabobs

This traditional and much-loved combination of flavors always works well on the barbecue.

 15 mins   🕐 8 mins

SERVES 4

I N G R E D I E N T S

1 lb/450 g thick ham steak

15 oz/425 g canned pineapple pieces in natural juice

8 oz/225 g firm Brie, chilled

2 tbsp sunflower oil

1 garlic clove, crushed

1 tbsp lemon juice

½ tsp ground nutmeg

¼ tsp ground cloves

pepper

freshly cooked rice, to serve

1 Cut the ham into even-size chunks. Place the chunks in a pan of boiling water and simmer for 5 minutes.

2 Drain the pineapple pieces and reserve 3 tablespoons of the juice. Cut the chilled cheese into large chunks.

3 To make the baste, put the reserved pineapple juice, oil, garlic, lemon juice, nutmeg, cloves, in a small screw-top jar, add pepper to taste, and shake until well combined. Set aside until required.

4 Remove the ham from the pan with a slotted spoon. Thread the ham onto skewers, alternating with the pineapple and cheese pieces.

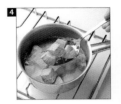

5 Grill the kabobs over warm coals, turning and basting frequently with the oil and pineapple juice mixture, for 2–4 minutes on each side, until the pineapple and ham are hot and the cheese is just beginning to melt. Do not overcook, otherwise the cheese will become runny and the kabobs will become a mess; allow enough time to reheat the ham and for the pineapple to warm through.

6 Remove the kabobs from the heat and serve on a bed of freshly cooked rice.

Ginger Beef with Chile

Serve these fruity, hot, spicy steaks with noodles. Use a nonstick, ridged grill pan to cook with a minimum of fat.

NUTRITIONAL INFORMATION

Calories	179	Sugars	.........8g
Protein	........21g	Fat	...........6g
Carbohydrate	....8g	Saturates	......2g

🍲 40 mins 🕐 10 mins

SERVES 4

I N G R E D I E N T S

4 lean beef steaks, such as rump, sirloin, or fillet, 3½ oz/100 g each

2 tbsp ginger wine

1-inch/2.5-cm piece of fresh gingerroot, finely chopped

1 garlic clove, crushed

1 tsp ground chili

1 tsp vegetable oil

salt and pepper

strips of fresh red chile, to garnish

T O   S E R V E

freshly cooked noodles

2 scallions, shredded

R E L I S H

8 oz/225 g fresh pineapple

1 small red bell pepper

1 fresh red chile

2 tbsp light soy sauce

1 piece of preserved ginger in syrup, drained and chopped

1 Trim any excess fat from the steaks if necessary. Using a meat mallet or covered rolling pin, pound the steaks until they are ½ inch/1 cm thick. Season on both sides with salt and pepper to taste and place in a shallow dish.

2 Combine the ginger wine, fresh gingerroot, garlic, and ground chili and pour over the meat. Cover with plastic wrap and chill for 30 minutes.

3 Meanwhile, make the relish. Peel and finely chop the pineapple and place it in a bowl. Halve, seed, and finely chop the bell pepper and chile. Stir into the pineapple with the soy sauce and preserved ginger. Cover with plastic wrap and chill until required.

4 Brush a ridged grill pan with the oil and heat until very hot. Drain the beef and add to the pan, pressing down to sear. Lower the heat and cook for 5 minutes. Turn the steaks over and cook for another 5 minutes.

5 Drain the steaks on paper towels and transfer to warmed serving plates. Garnish with chile strips and serve with noodles, scallions, and the relish.

Summer Puddings

A marvelous mixture of summer fruits encased in slices of white bread, which soak up all the deep red, flavorful juices.

NUTRITIONAL INFORMATION	
Calories 250	Sugars 41g
Protein 4g	Fat 4g
Carbohydrate ...53g	Saturates 2g

15 mins, plus chilling

5–10 mins

SERVES 6

I N G R E D I E N T S

vegetable oil or butter, for greasing

6–8 thin slices white bread, crusts removed

¾ cup superfine sugar

1¼ cups water

8 oz/225 g strawberries

1 lb/450 g raspberries

1¼ cups black currants and/or red currants

1½ cups blackberries or loganberries

sprigs of fresh mint, to decorate

light pouring cream, to serve

1 Grease 6 ⅔-cup molds with a little butter or oil.

2 Line the molds with the bread, cutting it so it fits snugly.

3 Place the sugar in a pan with the water and heat gently, stirring frequently, until dissolved, then bring to a boil and continue to boil for 2 minutes.

4 Reserve 6 large strawberries for decoration. Add half the remaining raspberries and the rest of the fruits to the syrup in the pan, cutting the strawberries in half if large, and simmer gently for a few minutes, until they are beginning to soften but still retain their shape.

5 Spoon the fruits and some of the liquid into the molds. Cover with more slices of bread. Spoon a little juice around the sides of the molds so the bread is well soaked. Cover with a saucer, place a heavy weight on top, then let cool and chill thoroughly, preferably overnight.

6 Process the remaining raspberries in a food processor or blender, or press through a nonmetallic strainer. Add enough of the liquid from the fruits to give a coating consistency.

7 Turn out the puddings onto serving plates and spoon over the raspberry sauce. Decorate with the mint sprigs and reserved strawberries and serve with cream.

Raspberry Fool

This dish is very easy to make and can be prepared
in advance and stored in the refrigerator until required.

NUTRITIONAL INFORMATION

Calories ....288 Sugars 19g
Protein ....4g Fat 22g
Carbohydrate ...19g Saturates 14g

1¼ hrs   0 mins

SERVES 4

INGREDIENTS

10½ oz/300 g fresh raspberries

6 tbsp confectioners' sugar

10 fl oz/300 ml crème fraîche or thick plain
 yogurt, plus extra to decorate

½ tsp vanilla extract

2 egg whites

raspberries and lemon balm leaves,
 to decorate

1 Put the raspberries and confectioners' sugar in a food processor or blender and process until smooth, or press through a strainer with the back of a spoon.

2 Reserve 1 tablespoon per portion of crème fraîche for decorating.

3 Put the remaining crème fraîche and the vanilla extract in a bowl and stir in the raspberry mixture.

4 Whisk the egg whites in a separate mixing bowl, until stiff peaks form. Gently fold the egg whites into the raspberry mixture using a metal spoon, until fully incorporated.

5 Spoon the raspberry fool into individual serving dishes and chill for at least 1 hour. Decorate with the reserved crème fraîche or yogurt, raspberries, and lemon balm leaves, and serve.

COOK'S TIP
Although this dessert is
best made with fresh raspberries
in season, an acceptable result
can be achieved with frozen
raspberries, which are available
from most food stores.

Mint-Chocolate Gelato

Rich, creamy gelati, or ice creams, are one of the great Italian culinary contributions to the world. This version is made with fresh mint.

NUTRITIONAL INFORMATION

Calories	575	Sugars	........53g
Protein	........17g	Fat	..........34g
Carbohydrate	...54g	Saturates	......18g

5–6 hrs 20 mins

SERVES 4

INGREDIENTS

6 large eggs

¾ cup superfine sugar

1¼ cups milk

⅔ cup heavy cream

large handful of fresh mint leaves, rinsed and dried

2 drops green food coloring, optional

2 oz/55 g dark chocolate, finely chopped

1 Put the eggs and sugar in a heatproof bowl that will sit over a pan with plenty of room underneath. Using an electric mixer, beat the eggs and sugar together, until thick and creamy.

2 Put the milk and cream in the pan and bring to a simmer, where small bubbles appear all around the edge, stirring. Pour onto the eggs, whisking constantly. Rinse the pan and put 1 inch/2.5 cm water in the bottom. Place the bowl on top, making sure the bottom does not touch the water. Turn the heat to medium–high and cook, stirring, for 1 minute.

3 Transfer the mixture to a pan and cook, stirring constantly, until it is thick enough to coat the back of the spoon and leave a mark when you pull your finger across it.

4 Tear the mint leaves and stir them into the custard. Remove the custard from the heat. Let cool, then cover and let infuse for at least 2 hours, chilling for the last 30 minutes.

5 Strain the mixture through a small nylon strainer to remove the pieces of mint. Stir in the food coloring, if using. Transfer to a freezer container and freeze the mixture for 1–2 hours, until frozen 1 inch/2.5 cm from the sides.

6 Scrape into a bowl and beat again until smooth. Stir in the chocolate pieces, smooth the top, and cover with plastic wrap or foil.

7 Freeze until set, for up to 3 months. Place in the refrigerator to soften for 20 minutes before serving.

Melon & Kiwi Salad

A refreshing fruit salad, ideal to serve after a rich meal. This recipe uses galia melon, but Charentais or cantaloupe melons are also good.

NUTRITIONAL INFORMATION

Calories	88	Sugars	........17g
Protein	.........1g	Fat	..........0.2g
Carbohydrate	...17g	Saturates	.......0g

1¼ hrs   0 mins

SERVES 4

I N G R E D I E N T S

½ galia melon

2 kiwifruit

18–20 white seedless grapes

1 papaya, halved

3 tbsp orange-flavored liqueur, such as Cointreau

1 tbsp chopped lemon verbena, lemon balm, or mint

sprigs of lemon verbena, or whole ground cherries, to decorate

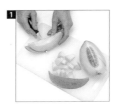  

1 Remove the seeds from the melon, cut it into 4 slices, and carefully cut away the skin. Cut the flesh into cubes and put into a bowl.

2 Peel the kiwifruit and cut across into slices. Add to the melon with the white grapes.

3 Remove the seeds from the papaya and cut off the skin. Slice the flesh thickly and cut into diagonal pieces. Add to the fruit bowl and mix well.

4 Mix together the liqueur and the chopped lemon verbena, pour over the fruit, and let macerate for 1 hour, stirring occasionally.

5 Spoon the fruit salad into glasses, pour over the juices, and then decorate with lemon verbena sprigs or ground cherries.

COOK'S TIP

Lemon balm or sweet balm is a fragrant lemon-scented plant with slightly hairy, serrated leaves and a pronounced lemon flavor. Lemon verbena can also be used—this has an even stronger lemon flavor and smooth, elongated leaves.

Balsamic Strawberries

Generations of Italian cooks have known that the unlikely combination of freshly ground black pepper and ripe, juicy strawberries is fantastic.

NUTRITIONAL INFORMATION

Calories	132	Sugars	.........5g
Protein	.........1g	Fat	..........12g
Carbohydrate	....5g	Saturates	.......7g

4¼ hrs

0 mins

SERVES 4–6

INGREDIENTS

1 lb/450 g fresh strawberries

2–3 tbsp balsamic vinegar

fresh mint leaves, torn, plus extra to decorate (optional)

½–¾ cup mascarpone cheese

pepper

1 Wipe the strawberries with a damp cloth, rather than rinsing them, so they do not become soggy. Using a paring knife, cut off the green stalks at the top and use the tip of the knife to remove the core or hull.

COOK'S TIP

This is most enjoyable when it is made with the best-quality balsamic vinegar, one that has aged slowly and has turned thick and syrupy. Unfortunately, the genuine mixture is always expensive. Less expensive versions are artificially sweetened and colored with caramel.

2 Cut each strawberry in half lengthwise or into fourths if large. Transfer to a bowl.

3 Add the balsamic vinegar, allowing ½ tablespoon per person. Add several twists of ground black pepper, then gently stir together. Cover with plastic wrap and chill for up to 4 hours.

4 Just before serving, stir in torn mint leaves to taste. Spoon the mascarpone into bowls and spoon the berries on top. Decorate with a few mint leaves, if desired. Sprinkle with extra pepper to taste.

Orange & Bitters Sherbet

Made from a distinctive Italian drink and freshly squeezed orange juice, this smooth, pale-pink sherbet is a cooling dessert with a refreshing tang.

NUTRITIONAL INFORMATION

Calories 212   Sugars 52g
Protein . . . . .2g   Fat 0g
Carbohydrate . . .52g   Saturates 0g

3 hrs   3–5 mins

SERVES 4–6

INGREDIENTS

3–4 large oranges

generous 1 cup superfine sugar

2½ cups water

3 tbsp red Italian bitters, such as Campari

2 extra-large egg whites

TO DECORATE

fresh mint leaves

candied citrus peel (optional)

4 Roll the 3 pared oranges back and forth on the counter, pressing them down firmly. Cut them in half and squeeze ½ cup of juice from them. If you need more juice, squeeze the remaining orange. When the syrup is cool, stir in the orange juice and bitters. Strain into a container, cover, and chill for at least 30 minutes.

5 Put the mixture in an ice-cream maker and churn for about 15 minutes. Alternatively, transfer to a freezerproof container and freeze for 1 hour, then place in a bowl and beat to break up the ice crystals. Put back in the container and freeze for 30 minutes. Repeat twice more, freezing for 30 minutes and whisking each time.

6 Whisk the egg whites in a clean, grease-free bowl, until stiff peaks form. Add the egg whites to the ice-cream maker and continue churning for 5 minutes, or add to the ice cream in a bowl, beat, freeze for 30 minutes, then beat again. Transfer to a shallow, freezerproof container, cover, and freeze for up to 2 months.

7 About 15 minutes before serving, place the ice cream in the refrigerator to soften, then scoop into bowls and serve decorated with mint leaves, and candied citrus peel if desired.

1 Working over a bowl to catch any juice, pare the zest from 3 of the oranges, without removing the bitter white pith. If some of the pith does come off with the zest, use the knife to scrape it off. Reserve the zest.

2 Put the sugar and water in a pan and stir over low heat, until dissolved. Increase the heat and boil for 2 minutes, without stirring. Using a wet pastry brush, brush any crystals down the side of the pan, if necessary.

3 Remove the pan from the heat and pour into a heatproof, nonmetallic bowl. Add the reserved orange zest and set aside to steep while the mixture cools to room temperature.

Lemon Granita

Soft and granular, this iced dessert has a sharp, zingy flavor, which is refreshing and ideal for rounding off any rich meal.

NUTRITIONAL INFORMATION

Calories 78   Sugars 20g
Protein . . . . .1g   Fat 0g
Carbohydrate . . .20g   Saturates 0g

4 hrs   5 mins

SERVES 4–6

INGREDIENTS

4 large unwaxed lemons

½ cup superfine sugar

3 cups water

scooped-out lemon shells, to serve (optional)

sprigs of fresh mint, to decorate (optional)

1 Pare 6 strips of rind from 1 of the lemons, then finely grate the remaining rind from the remaining lemons, being very careful not to remove any bitter white pith.

2 Roll the lemons back and forth on the counter, pressing down firmly. Cut each in half and squeeze ½ cup juice. Add the grated rind to the juice. Set aside.

VARIATION

Lemon-scented herbs add a unique and unexpected flavor. Add 4 small sprigs of lemon balm or 2 sprigs of lemon thyme to the syrup in step 3. Remove and discard with the pared rind in step 4. Or stir ½ tablespoon finely chopped lemon thyme into the mixture in step 4.

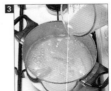
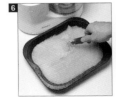

3 Put the pared strips of lemon rind, sugar, and water in a pan and stir over low heat to dissolve the sugar. Increase the heat and boil for 4 minutes, without stirring. Use a wet pastry brush to brush down any spatters on the side of the pan. Turn off the heat and stir in the lemon juice, then pour into a heatproof nonmetallic bowl and set aside to cool.

4 Remove the strips of rind from the syrup. Stir in the grated rind. Transfer to a shallow metal container, cover, and freeze for up to 3 months.

5 Chill serving bowls 30 minutes before serving. To serve, invert the container onto a cutting board. Rinse a cloth in very hot water, wring it out, then rub on the bottom of the container for 15 seconds. Give the container a shake and the mixture should fall out.

6 Break up the granita with a knife and then transfer to a food processor. Process until it becomes granular. Serve in the chilled bowls (or in scooped-out lemons). Decorate with sprigs of fresh mint, if desired.